B.F.F. Quizzes

Fun quizzes for you and your B.F.F.s!

T0125698

Movies!

⭐ **What would you rather watch?**
☐ *Brave*   ☐ *Ratatouille*   ☐ *Madagascar*

⭐ **Who are you most like?**
☐ Katniss Everdeen   ☐ Hermione Granger

⭐ **Disney movies are:**
☐ Too young for me!   ☐ The best movies ever made.

⭐ **What are you always in the mood for?**
☐ Comedy   ☐ Action!   ☐ Romance

⭐ **All-time favorite Disney princess:**
☐ Cinderella   ☐ Snow White   ☐ Sleeping Beauty

⭐ **Who would you rather be?**
☐ The villain   ☐ The sidekick   ☐ The hero

⭐ **Your least favorite sidekick:**
☐ Russell (*Up*)   ☐ Donkey (*Shrek*)   ☐ Dory (*Finding Nemo*)

★ **Classic movie that's still good today:**
☐ *The Sound of Music* ☐ *E.T.* ☐ *Mary Poppins*

★ **Your favorite movie character is:**
☐ A real person ☐ A cartoon

★ **Best time of day to watch a flick:**
☐ Morning ☐ Afternoon ☐ Night

★ **Where would you rather watch a movie?**
☐ Movie theater ☐ Home ☐ Friend's house

★ **Which are you:**
☐ Team Jacob ☐ Team Edward

★ **Would you rather:**
☐ Be in a movie ☐ Write the screenplay

★ **Which Marvel movie is best?**
☐ *Iron Man* ☐ *Spiderman* ☐ *X-Men*

★ **Fave movie theater food:**
☐ Popcorn ☐ Licorice ☐ Slurpee

ADMIT ONE

ADMIT ONE

ADMIT ONE

3

What's your ideal vacation spot?

Do you enjoy camping near a lake? How about taking a sunset stroll on the beach? Maybe you get a thrill from the sights and sounds of the city. Take this quiz to help you determine your ideal vacation spot.

1 When packing for a vacation you:
   a. Bring the bare minimum in a small duffle bag.
   b. Fill a small suitcase with bathing suits only.
   c. Fill two suitcases with your entire wardrobe.

2 Which song best describes your personality?
   a. "Home on the Range"
   b. "California Girls"
   C. "New York, New York"

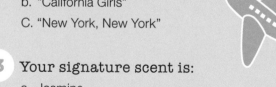

3 Your signature scent is:
   a. Jasmine
   b. Amber
   c. Green Apple

4 Your footwear for the summer consists of:

    a. Sneakers! You're an active girl.

    b. Footwear? You go barefoot!

    c. Some cute, sparkly flats.

5 How long does it take you to get ready each morning?

    a. 10 minutes

    b. 30 minutes

    c. At least 1 hour

6 If you could be described in one word, it would be:

    a. Organic. You have a connection with nature.

    b. Cool. Nothing gets to you.

    c. Glamorous. Your live for art and fashion.

7 Your ideal dog would be a:

    a. German Shepherd

    b. Cairn Terrier

    c. Poodle

8 Your dream house is a:

  a. Log cabin on a lake.

  b. A house on the beach.

  c. A brownstone in the city.

9 What do you want to be when you grow up?

  a. An environmental scientist

  b. A marine biologist

  c. A fashion designer

10 Your ideal birthday gift is:

  a. A new fishing pole

  b. A surf board

  c. A designer bag

VACATION
ANSWERS!

Mostly As:

Wyoming

Pitch that tent and get that campfire roaring! By nature you're an outdoorsy girl, which makes the country your ideal vacation spot. The sun and sand is nice, but nothing makes you happier than sleeping under a blanket of stars, roasting marshmallows, and listening to nature with the people who are most important to you. You find it fun and rewarding to hike by day, and fish for your dinner by night. You will love enjoy the open air, far from crowds and the stress of everyday life.

Maui

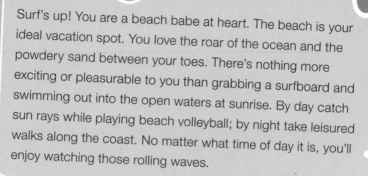

Surf's up! You are a beach babe at heart. The beach is your ideal vacation spot. You love the roar of the ocean and the powdery sand between your toes. There's nothing more exciting or pleasurable to you than grabbing a surfboard and swimming out into the open waters at sunrise. By day catch sun rays while playing beach volleyball; by night take leisured walks along the coast. No matter what time of day it is, you'll enjoy watching those rolling waves.

New York City

Noise, lights, action! The city is your ideal vacation spot. You love the hustle and bustle of urban life. Traveling by foot and catching cabs is your ideal way of getting around. You love to shop, dine, dance, and have a true appreciation for culture. Your perfect day is strolling through museums, grabbing a bite to eat from a gourmet food truck, and window shopping along busy city streets. At night, you'll enjoy dressing to the nine's and hitting the street in style.

Which holiday are you?

Holidays are a time of celebrating with those you love... and oftentimes an excuse to miss a day of school! Are you jolly like Christmas? Love things that go bump in the night? See which special occasion best suits your personality with this holiday quiz!

1 Which holiday celebration symbol is your favorite?
   a. Christmas tree with all the trimmings.
   b. Jack-o-Lantern with crooked teeth.
   c. White lilies draped over a pink basket.

2 Which holiday figure do you like best?
   a. Rudolph
   b. Dracula
   c. A peculiar bunny who likes to hide things.

3 In which season do you feel the most festive?
   a. Winter
   b. Autumn
   c. Spring

4 Which holiday meal sounds most delicious to you?

a. Roast turkey dinner with yule log dessert.

b. Chili, corn bread, and candy.

c. Ham and fancy tarts.

5 Which clothing article would you rather wear?

a. A red tulle skirt.

b. An outrageous costume.

c. Floral print dress with matching gloves.

6 Your best friend had a bad day and needs cheering up. How do you help?

a. Secretly leave her a gift.

b. Play a harmless prank on her – laughter is the best medicine!

c. Bake her a batch of cookies, decorated of course!

7 Which of the following songs do you like best?

a. "Jingle Bell Rock"

b. "Monster Mash"

c. Any church song

8 Of the following color schemes what's your favorite?

    a. Red, green, gold, and silver

    b. Orange, black, purple, and green

    c. White, pink, yellow, and purple

9 Which of the following flavors and smells do you prefer?

    a. Gingerbread & cinnamon

    b. Cider & fresh pumpkin

    c. Fresh flowers & chocolate

10 Which holiday activity is your favorite when preparing a celebration?

    a. Decorating the house.

    b. Plotting your next trick.

    c. Coloring eggs.

HOLIDAY ANSWERS!

Mostly As

Christmas Cheer

Year round you look forward to warm and cozy gatherings, traditional eats, and familiar faces. You are likely to spread a lot of joy during the Christmas season. You enjoy giving gifts and making the day special for all of your loved ones.

Mostly Bs

Spirit of Halloween

You enjoy silly fun, sweet treats, and spooky surprises. You are most likely to have more fun than most on this eerie holiday, and your costumes are certainly the spookiest. You enjoy collecting candy as much as you enjoy sharing it.

Mostly Cs

Spring Flinger

Easter holiday excites you most, not just because of the special meaning behind the day, but also the beauty of spring weather. You enjoy simplicity and newness, like fresh young flowers on a sunny afternoon. Of course, the exciting hunt for eggs and baskets of candy are nice too!

11

What's your music personality?

Rock on! Music has the power to instantly transform the way you feel. Whether you love hip-hop or old rock 'n' roll, everyone has a genre of music that they can connect to! Take this quiz to help determine what type of music best describes you.

1 **When you are at your school dance, you:**
a. Dance to a choreographed routine.
b. Let the music move you.
c. Sway side to side.

2 **Your hair is:**
a. Dyed pink at the tips
b. Sleek and straight
c. Worn in loose waves

3 **What are your go-to pair of shoes?**
a. Glitter derby shoes
b. Black patent sneakers
c. Cowboy boots

4 When you wear a hat, you choose:
   a. A black fedora
   b. A cool visor
   c. A floppy straw hat

5 Your favorite sport is:
   a. Cheerleading
   b. Basketball
   c. Football

6 When do you wear makeup?
   a. All the time!
   b. When you feel like it!
   c. Hardly ever!

7 If you could be an ice cream flavor, you'd be:
   a. Birthday Cake
   b. Chocolate Caramel
   c. Butter Pecan

8 Where is your ideal vacation spot?
- a. Los Angeles
- b. New York City
- c. Dallas

9 You are most likely to be voted:
- a. Most Talkative
- b. Best Dressed
- c. Sweetest Friend

10 Your favorite season is:
- a. Summer
- b. Winter
- c. Fall

Pop

Mostly As:

You're not sure what it is about pop music that gets your body grooving! Maybe it's the catchy lyrics or the mix of rhythm and beats that mesmerize you. You secretly (or not so secretly) idolize Lady Gaga, Katy Perry, and Justin Bieber, and are frequently caught in class humming the chorus of the top pop songs from the Billboard Top 100 Countdown. You admire pop culture and probably even own an MJ jacket and/or have Katy Perry-inspired blue locks.

Hip Hop R&B

Mostly Bs:

You are cool, calm, and smooth at all times... which is why hip-hop is your music type. You're in tune to the edgy beats of artists like Drake, Rihanna, and B.O.B. When hanging out with friends or your crush, let the smooth beats of your fave hip-hop/R&B groups set the tone. Hip-hop music is great for dancing or thinking, two things you love to do!

Country

Mostly Cs:

You are a country girl at heart! This genre resonates with you because you enjoy lyrics that have a light, playful or deep meaning. Plus your love for rural living helps you appreciate the message and settings of these down-home, back country tunes. Sport your cowboy boots and straw hat while singing along to Taylor Swift, Carrie Underwood, and Kenny Chesney.

Back to School

- Your school friends are:
  ☐ Just like you ☐ Totally different

- Subject you like least:
  ☐ Social Studies ☐ Math ☐ Science

- Your teacher is:
  ☐ So nice! ☐ A real meanie

- What's worse?
  ☐ Class presentation ☐ Homework

- Speaking in front of the class is:
  ☐ Nerve-wracking ☐ Exciting!

- You'd rather:
  ☐ Read a book ☐ Write a story

- What are you better at?
  ☐ Division ☐ Multiplication

Your favorite time of day is:
☐ P.E. ☐ Recess!

What best describes you?
☐ Class clown ☐ Ms. Popular ☐ Well-liked

Favorite school attire is:
☐ Cool pants & top ☐ Cute dress ☐ Changes every day

Ever cheated?
☐ Never! ☐ Maybe…

Troublemaker or teacher's pet?
☐ Troublemaker ☐ Teacher's pet

School is a place to:
☐ Socialize ☐ Learn

Passing notes in class is:
☐ Fun ☐ Immature

Recess is a time for:
☐ Gossiping with GFs ☐ Activities!

2+3=

Which school subject are you?

Believe it or not, your favorite school subject speaks volumes about your personality. Are you a creative or practical thinker? Do you prefer to learn through reading and writing, or do you like a more hands-on approach? Take this quiz to help you decide which school subject you are!

1 When you help put away the groceries you:

a. Put items away in alphabetical order.

b. Put them in any cabinet.

c. Put them in specific areas.

2 What is your room full of?

a. Checklists and sticky notes

b. Books and magazines

c. Pets and projects

3 You learn best by using your:

a. Ears

b. Eyes

c. Hands

4 What would be the best gift to give to you?

    a. A new graphing calculator.

    b. A subscription to *InStyle*.

    c. A dissection kit.

5 What's your ideal after-school activity?

    a. Future Business Leaders of America

    b. Debate Team

    c. Environmental Club

6 Mixing chemicals in science class is:

    a. Pretty cool

    b. Not your thing

    c. All you care about

7 Learning about the works of Shakespeare is:

    a. Beyond boring

    b. Beyond fascinating

    c. Important to understand

8 **Solving proofs:**

a. Makes you happy.

b. Is frustrating.

c. Is simple but boring.

9 **What do you do before you run errands?**

a. Make a list of places to go in order of importance.

b. Enjoy yourself and take your time.

c. Make a mental list of what you need.

10 **You think the school should spend more money on:**

a. Smart boards

b. School play costumes

c. New lab materials

Mostly As:

Math: You are systematic, organized, and thoughtful. You like creating checklists of things to do and completing them in order. If you have a lot on your plate, you are great at calmly tackling one thing at a time. You have a way with numbers and can quickly calculate a percentage in your mind on your shopping excursions. You're a practical thinker who finds joy in helping friends find solutions to their problems.

Mostly Bs:

English: You are a deep thinker. Similar to the study of literature, you enjoy analyzing people and finding the hidden meaning in your relationships. You have a vast imagination and get lost in it regularly. You can never get enough of the written word, and often browse the Internet for news, peruse magazines for fashion trends, and download the New York Times' bestsellers list of books on your Kindle.

Mostly Cs:

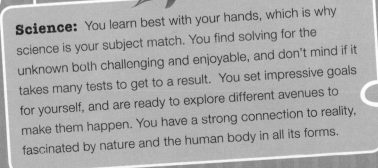

Science: You learn best with your hands, which is why science is your subject match. You find solving for the unknown both challenging and enjoyable, and don't mind if it takes many tests to get to a result. You set impressive goals for yourself, and are ready to explore different avenues to make them happen. You have a strong connection to reality, fascinated by nature and the human body in all its forms.

Does he want to be more than friends?

He loves you, he loves you not? If you have your eye on someone special, you want to know if he feels the same way. Take this quiz to help you determine if he wants to be more than friends!

1 When you wear an outfit that complements your best features, he:

a. Slips you a note saying you look pretty.

b. Says you look nice and gives you a high five.

c. Says hi as you switch classes.

2 You curl your hair for school. He:

a. Notices immediately!

b. Notices at the end of the day.

c. Did not look at you today.

3 You ask your crush to dance. He:

a. Jumps up and says, "Absolutely!"

b. Shrugs and says, "Sure."

c. Says, "OK," but dances with another girl the rest of the night.

4 You both end up partners for a science project. He:

   a. Makes sure he does equal work.

   b. Slacks off slightly.

   c. Doesn't do any work at all.

5 Your pencil breaks during class. What does he do?

   a. Hands you his only pencil.

   b. Says, "Tough Break!"

   c. Doesn't notice!

6 For Halloween he suggests you be:

   a. A bride

   b. A nurse

   c. A witch

7 Your school is sponsoring a carnation fundraiser for Valentine's Day. He:

   a. Sends you a red one.

   b. Sends you a pink one.

   c. Sends you nothing.

8 If he had to use a word to describe you, it's:

  a. Perfection

  b. Fun

  c. Dependable

9 You compliment him on his science presentation. He:

  a. Blushes instantly!

  b. Says, "Thanks buddy!"

  c. Smiles and nods.

10 In gym class, he:

  a. Picks you first.

  b. Picks you after his buds.

  c. Does not pick you at all.

LOVE
ANSWERS!

Mostly As

Without a Doubt! Yes! He is over the top, head over heels for you! He's gone out of his way to make you notice him, and wants to treat you right in a big way. He is someone you can trust, spend time with, and maybe even fall in love with eventually. When you're together you share a romantic attraction because you have similar interests and aspirations. This is a match made in heaven!

Mostly Bs

It's Very Possible!

Maybe! He likes you but is unsure if it's in a romantic way. You are undoubtedly good friends, and there is potential for more once you get to know each other better. You both have similar interests, but spending time with his guy friends is more of a priority than having a girlfriend. Take things slowly, and maybe you'll both feel a spark when the time is right.

Mostly Cs

Just Friends!

It looks like this guy sees you as a friend. This may feel like a bummer now, but it doesn't seem like he treats you as well as you deserve to be treated anyway. Be there as a friend for him, but don't put him on a pedestal. Wait for a guy who makes it clear he thinks you are perfect to him, one who is respectful, sweet, and thoughtful. It's time to move on to other fish in the sea.

Who's your celeb style match?

Are you constantly perusing magazines to learn the latest fashion trends, or do you enjoy creating your own? Take this quiz and see which celeb shares your fab sense of style!

1 Your go-to make up item is:
   a. Pink lip gloss
   b. Black eyeliner
   c. Chapstick

2 The school dance is coming up. What will you wear?
   a. A pink strapless dress
   b. A tight, black dress
   c. A striped maxi dress

3 What type of music do you enjoy the most?
   a. Country
   b. Heavy Metal
   c. Alternative

4 Your ideal dog is a:

a. Yorkie

b. Pit bull

c. Bulldog

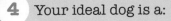

5 What is your favorite store?

a. Forever 21

b. Hot Topic

c. Urban Outfitters

6 Your favorite colors are:

a. Pink and purple

b. Black and grey

c. Brown and Red

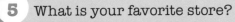

7 Who is your celebrity crush?

a. Justin Bieber

b. Chace Crawford

c. Robert Pattinson

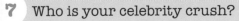

8 For Halloween you dress up as a:

a. Princess

b. Rocker

c. Vampire

9 What is your favorite ride at a theme park?

a. The carousel

b. Bumper cars

c. Flying swings

10 If you could be any candy you would be:

a. A Hershey Kiss

b. Hot Tamales

c. Twizzlers

ACTION!!!

Mostly As

Emma Roberts

You are flirty and feminine, and you show this through your outfits just like Emma Roberts. You adore frilly mini skirts and fluttery cap sleeves. Pink is your signature color and it suits you well. You like classic accessories like gold hoops and diamond studs, and there has never been a peep toe pump you did not love!

Mostly Bs

Taylor Momsen

You have a chic edge to the way you look and dress, just like Taylor Momsen. You have a rocker, edgy vibe about you, and you don't care about any criticisms from your parents. You like leather, button-up vests, and tighter than tight skinny jeans. Derby shoes are your go-to footwear and you regularly wear fedoras and Ray Bans.

Mostly Cs

Kristen Stewart

You dress for comfort, not style, putting you in the Boho chic category with Kristen Stewart. Loose fitting tunics and floor length skirts make you feel most comfortable. You keep jewelry to a minimum, but when you do wear it, you opt for long, layered chains or leather wrap bracelets. You enjoy a flat strappy sandal or colorful flip flops, and you keep your hair pulled back.

Sports

❀ **You would rather:**
- ☐ Play football ☐ Cheer on the sidelines

❀ **What's better?**
- ☐ Real Basketball ☐ Nerf basketball

❀ **What's more fun?**
- ☐ Tennis ☐ Ping Pong

❀ **What's easier?**
- ☐ Handstand ☐ Roundoff

❀ **Which sport is better?**
- ☐ Soccer ☐ Lacrosse

❀ **Which activity do you enjoy most?**
- ☐ Bike riding ☐ Skateboarding ☐ Rollerblading

❀ **You're more likely to be MVP for:**
- ☐ NBA ☐ MLB

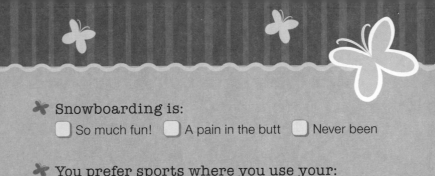

Snowboarding is:
☐ So much fun! ☐ A pain in the butt ☐ Never been

You prefer sports where you use your:
☐ Hands ☐ Feet ☐ Head

Beach activity you prefer:
☐ Volleyball ☐ Paddle Ball ☐ Surfing

Which is worse?
☐ Golf ☐ Track & Field

Flag football is:
☐ Fun ☐ Too rough for you!

Best position in baseball:
☐ Catcher ☐ Pitcher ☐ The stand

You're more likely to be:
☐ Backup dancer ☐ Lead performer ☐ Choreographer

Dance you'd rather learn:
☐ Ballet ☐ Hip Hop ☐ Jazz

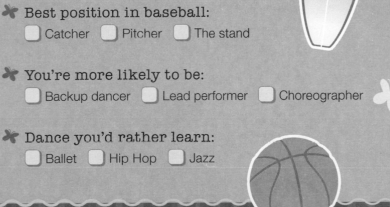

Which classic movie are you?

Classic movies are oldies but goodies. They're packed full of character, action, and of course, old fashioned romance. Take this quiz to help you learn which classic movie you would be!

1 Which word best describes you?
a. Determined
b. Tough
c. Charming

2 You think love is:
a. Everlasting
b. Not for you
c. Necessary

3 Which fruit or veggie would you be?
a. A lemon
b. A hot pepper
c. A peach

4 What is your favorite color?
  a. Yellow
  b. Black
  c. Pink

5 You live in the:
  a. Country
  b. Suburbs
  c. City

6 What is your favorite musical instrument?
  a. The piano
  b. The guitar
  c. The flute

7 You think the most stylish decade is:
  a. The 1800s
  b. The 1950s
  c. The 1960s

8 If you could own any pet you would own a:

a. Horse

b. Cat

c. Poodle

9 Which color nail polish would you choose?

a. Nude

b. Black

c. Red

10 Your classic celebrity crush is:

a. Clark Gable

b. James Dean

c. James Stewart

Gone with the Wind

MOSTLY As

You are a free spirit who has a tremendous amount of determination. No matter how many times you fall, you get right back up, much like the theme of *Gone with the Wind*. People like to be around you because you are sassy but sweet. You are charming, social, and outspoken, much like the movie's main character, Scarlett O'Hara.

Rebel Without a Cause

MOSTLY Bs

You are edgy, rebellious, and stand up for what you believe in, even if it means challenging authority. You're not a fan of limiting social conventions and attract other free-thinkers, like Jim Stark in *Rebel Without a Cause*. You don't care about popularity, but prefer to have a few very close friends who truly understand you. You are the type of person who will change the world.

Breakfast at Tiffany's

MOSTLY Cs

You're a dreamer, just like Holly Golightly in *Breakfast at Tiffany's*. You enjoy the finer things in life and make sure you get them. You are a social butterfly, hosting the best get-togethers, and take pride in your appearance. You have many male suitors that are head over heels for you, thanks to your hard-to-get strategy and striking presence.

What type of friend are you?

Friends: We all want them and we all need them. Have you ever taken a step back to consider what type of friend you are to others? Take this quiz and find out!

1 Your friend can't open her locker and is going to be late. You:

   a. Stay to help her (and are late too).

   b. Kick it until it opens for her.

   c. Make her laugh while you pry it open.

2 Your friend forgets her deodorant for gym class. You:

   a. Offer up yours.

   b. Check to see if anyone has an extra.

   c. Jokingly tell her she smells!

3 There is a huge birthday bash this weekend. You:

   a. Roll up with your girls!

   b. Jog to the party.

   c. Show up late in a crazy outfit.

4 Your friend's boyfriend is flirting with you. You:

   a. Tell her right away!
   b. Tell him you know karate.
   c. Embarrass him in public.

5 In school you are most likely to be voted:

   a. Most Likely to Succeed
   b. Most Athletic
   c. The Class Clown

6 What is your ideal birthday present?

   a. A spa day with friends
   b. New workout gear
   c. The Office Season 4 DVDs

7 How do you cheer up a friend who is feeling blue?

   a. Bring her flowers.
   b. Take her to your Zumba class.
   c. Tell her a funny joke.

8 Your friend gets dumped. You:

   a. Bake her cookies.

   b. Go shopping with her.

   c. Make a list of his worst qualities.

9 What is your favorite activity to do with friends?

   a. Cooking

   b. Running

   c. Watching movies

10 Where do you plan on going with friends this summer?

   a. The beach

   b. A water park

   c. An amusement park

You + Me = B.F.F.

Mostly As:

A Soul Sister

You are a friend for life. You take friendships very seriously and choose your friends wisely. You go out of your way to make others feel special and appreciated. You send flowers on birthdays and "Get Well Soon" cards if your friends are home sick. You can be trusted with secrets and trust others as well. You are popular because you make and keep friends easily.

Mostly Bs:

An Active Friend

You can rarely sit still and that is what your friends love most about you. You get your girls up and moving, and can always be counted on for a new adventure. Whether you go shopping, hiking, or swimming, you are the friend that inspires others. Your constant energy and excitement for life motivates your gal pals to set and achieve their goals!

Mostly Cs:

A Funny Friend

You are like a ray of sunshine that makes everyone around you beam with smiles! That is why your friends consider you to be a funny friend. They can turn to you for the best jokes and one-liners that help them de-stress when things get tough. You are a good listener, and tend to make everyone feel better with your humor and sharp wit.

Which TV show best describes your life?

You watch TV not only because it's entertaining, but because you can relate to a character, a family, or a lifestyle. Take this quiz to help you figure out which TV show describes your life the best!

1 **You have to choose between your friend's party and your family reunion. You:**
   a. Pick the party, of course!
   b. Spend time with the family.
   c. Attend both!

2 **Your favorite musical is:**
   a. *Chicago*
   b. *The Lion King*
   c. *Grease*

3 **If you could be a chocolate candy, you would be:**
   a. A Peppermint Patty
   b. A Kit Kat
   c. An Almond Joy

4 If your siblings needed a ride home from school, you would:

  a. Make them walk.

  b. Be annoyed but do it.

  c. Happily do so.

5 How do you feel when your family fights?

  a. You don't know — you never see your parents.

  b. Totally normal.

  c. Unhappy but optimistic.

6 Is having a crush on your best friend's boyfriend ok?

  a. Definitely!

  b. Maybe?

  c. No way!

7 Where can you be found hanging out?

  a. A dance club

  b. A burger joint

  c. Choir practice

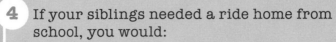

8 Would you ever sneak out of your house?
   a. I do it regularly.
   b. If I could get away with it, I would.
   c. Never!

9 Your go-to snack is:
   a. Sparkling water and olives
   b. A burger and fries
   c. Chips and dip

10 How would you describe your style?
   a. Posh and trendy
   b. Casual
   c. Individualistic

TV
ANSWERS!

Mostly As:

Gossip Girl

Your life closely resembles the plot and characters on *Gossip Girl*. You love the city and live for fashion, parties, and high society. You have many friends and even keep your enemies close by. You live for gossip and are a self-proclaimed drama queen. There is never a dull moment with your schoolmates, family, and social circle.

Mostly Bs:

Modern Family

You've learned that there is no right way to live life and love your "crazy" family. You are very close with every family member, despite your sometimes silly disagreements. With the unconditional love and support from your family and friends, you are sure to grow into a person of character.

Mostly Cs:

Glee

You are cheerful and are always humming a tune. In fact, music is the biggest part of your life. You have a close circle of friends who support your decisions, and most importantly, always encourage you to be yourself. You work hard and strive to be the best you can be in school and after-school activities.

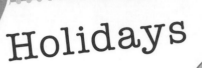 

Holidays

💜 **Valentine's Day is:**
☐ So lame ☐ Totally fun ☐ Only fun with friends

💜 **Your favorite holiday is in:**
☐ Spring ☐ Winter ☐ Fall

💜 **What's tastier?**
☐ Candy hearts ☐ Gingerbread cookies

💜 **Do you wear green on St. Patrick's Day?**
☐ Of course! ☐ If I remember to

💜 **You would rather decorate:**
☐ Gingerbread men ☐ Easter eggs

💜 **Thanksgiving is a time for:**
☐ Feasting! ☐ Spending time with family

💜 **New Year's is:**
☐ Way past your bedtime ☐ An excuse to dress up!

You would rather:
☐ Give gifts ☐ Receive gifts

Who gives better Christmas gifts?
☐ Santa ☐ Mom & Dad

How long is your Christmas list?
☐ Barely a page ☐ 2 pages, front and back

Which holiday is more fun?
☐ Halloween ☐ Valentine's Day

Your Halloween pumpkin is usually:
☐ Scary ☐ Goofy

Which would you rather be for Halloween?
☐ Disney character ☐ Superhero

The best part of 4th of July:
☐ Sparklers ☐ Epic firework show ☐ Parade

Ever given a Valentine to a boy you like?
☐ Yes ☐ No

Are you a good daughter?

Sometimes a mom or dad can be your best friend. Other times you just can't see eye to eye. Take this quiz to help you determine if you are a good daughter or not!

1 How often do you argue with your parents?
   a. Rarely
   b. Pretty often
   c. Too many times in a day to count

2 When asked to do dishes, you:
   a. Do them!
   b. Reluctantly do them.
   c. Laugh and leave the room.

3 The best present you gave your mom was:
   a. A locket with your picture.
   b. A gift card.
   c. A macaroni necklace when you were 5.

4 If a dress on your mom did not flatter her, you would:

   a. Subtly suggest a different outfit.

   b. Flat out tell her.

   c. Make fun of her.

5 What do you do when running late for curfew?

   a. Call right away.

   b. Call an hour late.

   c. Don't call at all.

6 You get a bad grade on a test. You:

   a. Confess and apologize.

   b. Shrug it off, and only tell them when questioned.

   c. Rip up the test. They'll never know.

7 Would you make plans on your dad's birthday?

   a. Never!

   b. It depends on the plans.

   c. You wouldn't think twice.

8 Your parents want to hang out with you on a Friday night. You:

a. Totally agree. It'll be fun.

b. Say yes. It's only one night.

c. Laugh and find something better to do.

9 You are asked to feed the cat while your parents go out of town. You:

a. Say, "No problem!"

b. Reluctantly agree.

c. Agree, but forget!

10 Your dad gets you an ugly jacket for your birthday. You:

a. Wear it right away.

b. Thank him, but hide it.

c. Force him to return it.

GOOD DAUGHTER
ANSWERS!

Yes, the best!

Mostly As:

You are a mommy and daddy's girl! Your parents are not only your guardians, they are your best friends. You would do anything for them. You help around the house without being asked. You don't make plans with friends at times, just so you can spend time with them. You always have the most thoughtful presents picked out for them, and you constantly strive to make them proud.

Yes, when you try!

Mostly Bs:

This is a complicated time for you and your parents—and that's totally normal. Sometimes you bump heads because you can't agree. You like their company, but enjoy hanging with your friends more. You occasionally forget to do your chores, or forget their birthdays. This does not mean you love them any less. Don't worry, you are a good daughter overall. Just remember to be respectful and show them you love them.

Keep working at it!

Mostly Cs:

Things can be rough between you and your parents during your teen years. It may seem like they're the enemy right now. Just remember everyone goes through this awkward time, and your parents are the ones who care about you the most. You can help by respecting the rules and helping around the house. Hanging with your friends is fun, but spending some quality time with your parents is important too. Take baby steps to build a stronger bond with them.

What's your signature style?

Everyone's style is slightly different and makes him or her unique. Whether you're a glamour girl, an edgy rocker, or a bohemian hipster, your signature style says a lot about you. Take this quiz to determine your signature style.

1 **When getting dressed for school you:**
a. Already have your clothes laid out.
b. Grab any top and bottom you see.
c. Dress around the day's events.

2 **If you could get any item for free, what would it be?**
a. An argyle sweater
b. An embellished scarf
c. A leather jacket

3 **What will your prom dress be?**
a. Sweet and pristine
b. A pants suit
c. Black, short, and tight

4 On the weekends, you:
   a. Work out.
   b. Read at the park.
   c. Shop with friends.

5 Your dream college is:
   a. Harvard
   b. Berkeley
   c. New York University

6 Where is your ideal vacation spot?
   a. The Hamptons
   b. San Francisco
   c. Miami

7 What would you most likely be on Halloween?
   a. A ballerina
   b. A hippie
   c. A pop star

8 Your go-to hair accessory is a:
   a. Ribbon
   b. Flower
   c. Peacock feather

9 Your school activities include:
   a. Honor Society
   b. Ecology Club
   c. Drama Club

10 If you could be a fruit or veggie you'd be:
   a. A shiny apple
   b. Anything organic
   c. A hot pepper

STYLE ANSWERS!

Mostly As:

Polished and Preppy

You are probably on the cheerleading squad or an officer in the student government. You love wearing classic pieces that never go out of style. You consider shopping a time to add investment pieces to your wardrobe. You admire clothing trends but rarely wear them. Neutral colored scarves, cardigans, khakis, oversized canvas monogram bags, and pearls are your go-to items.

Mostly Bs:

Hipster Chic

You dress for comfort and ease, and you exude confidence no matter what you wear. You are a fan of organic pieces, because you care about the environment more than making a fashion statement. You enjoy the basics—stripes, tanks, tees, jeans, and flowing skirts. You are usually spotted in a breezy maxi dress, thick strappy sandals, and some moonstone jewelry.

Mostly Cs:

Bold and Edgy

You are bold and beautiful. Always keeping up with the latest trends (or even starting them!), you like to put your own unique spin on the outfits you put together. You are known to mix modern pieces with vintage accessories. Leather jackets, skinny jeans, leggings, silk tank tops, mini skirts, body hugging dresses, and statement necklaces are your everyday pieces.

What's your makeup personality?

Makeup can be fun to some, necessary for others, and scary to a few. You have your own unique makeup style and method. Take this quiz to help you determine what your makeup personality is!

1 If you could only use one item forever, what would it be?

a. Red lipstick

b. Mascara

c. Moisturizer

2 Do you know how to apply makeup?

a. Of course! Any product, anywhere.

b. I know the basics.

c. Not a clue.

3 Makeup on runway models looks:

a. Amazing! So chic!

b. Ok, since they are on stage.

c. Ridiculous!

4 If you get a blemish, you:

   a. Instantly conceal it.

   b. Put an ice cube on it.

   c. Let it heal on its own.

5 Where do you buy your makeup?

   a. Sephora

   b. CVS

   c. I don't wear any!

6 What would you be for Halloween?

   a. Lady Gaga

   b. A cat

   c. A hippie

7 Your favorite color is:

   a. Pink

   b. Blue

   c. White

8 **What does your dream prom dress look like?**

a. Puffy and pink

b. Long and flowing

c. Casual and comfortable

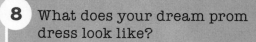

9 **When giving a presentation in class, you:**

a. Put on extra makeup, including fake lashes and glitter.

b. Stick to your normal makeup routine.

c. Apply chapstick to stay moisturized.

10 **What do you want to be when you grow up?**

a. A fashion designer

b. A lawyer

c. A teacher

Mostly As: All Dolled Up

To you, wearing makeup is creating new art forms on your face. You love coming up with a new dramatic look every day and piling it on! You adore lush, red lips and darkly lined eyes. You have a whole bag full of different shades and tones. Whether you are going to school, a dance, or out to get the mall, your face is always ready to get noticed!

Mostly Bs: Fresh Faced & Fabulous

You prefer to save bright makeup for special occasions, like the time you were in your cousin's wedding or went to the winter formal. On most days, you love a fresh faced look, making your skin glow and eyes sparkle using the fewest products possible. A swipe of mascara, a dab of blush, and a little bronzer is your go-to beauty regimen each morning.

Mostly Cs: Au Natural

Makeup looks nice on others, but it's not for you. You prefer a bare palette and find the secret to beauty is a natural face with healthy, glowing skin. You are proud of your looks and don't need anything to help you stand out. You make sure your skin is kept in tiptop shape with sun block, chapstick, and plenty of water throughout the day.

Places

🦋 **You would rather go to:**
☐ The beach ☐ The mountains

🦋 **What's better?**
☐ City ☐ Country

🦋 **Lake or ocean?**
☐ Lake ☐ Ocean

🦋 **What would you rather stay in?**
☐ Tent ☐ Luxury suite

🦋 **What would be more fun?**
☐ Hiking in a rainforest ☐ An African safari

🦋 **Which city would be more exciting?**
☐ Paris ☐ Rio de Janeiro ☐ New York

🦋 **Airplanes are:**
☐ Scary ☐ Fun!

You would rather:
☐ Cruise the Grand Canal in Venice   ☐ Ski in the Alps

How do you prefer to travel?
☐ By train   ☐ By plane   ☐ By boat

Which country seems most interesting?
☐ Germany   ☐ Spain   ☐ China

Has the best food?
☐ Tokyo   ☐ Mexico   ☐ Italy

Which would you rather do?
☐ Deep-sea fishing in Iceland   ☐ Snorkeling in Hawaii

Best spot for a vacation home:
☐ Ireland   ☐ Switzerland   ☐ Jamaica

Amusement park would you rather go to:
☐ Disneyland   ☐ Universal Studios

Speak more than 1 language?
☐ Ci, Oui, Danke - Yes!   ☐ Maybe someday

Which famous athlete are you?

There are numerous athletes today that excel in their own ways in different sports. You may resemble one of these top athletes by the way you act, the sport you play, or your personal style. Take this quiz to help you determine which famous athlete you are most like.

1 Which sport do you enjoy watching the most?
  a. Gymnastics
  b. Tennis
  c. Softball

2 You personal style is:
  a. A mix of sporty and girly.
  b. Athletic and comfortable.
  c. Stylish and flirty.

3 When something doesn't go your way, you:
  a. Keep trying!
  b. Get even more motivated.
  c. Accept it, but set a new goal.

4 How would you describe your body?

a. Muscular and petite

b. Tall and muscular

c. Slim and toned

5 What is your favorite food?

a. Salad

b. Seafood

c. Chicken

6 You are most likely to be voted:

a. Most Friendly

b. Most Athletic

c. Homecoming Queen

7 How often do you wear makeup?

a. Usually

b. Occasionally

c. Daily

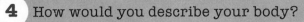

8 Which best describes your dating style?
a. Shy and quiet
b. Boastful and talkative
c. Flirty and outgoing

9 Which swimsuit would you choose?
a. A tankini
b. A one piece
c. A tiny bikini

10 Your hair is usually:
a. Pulled back
b. Braided
c. Worn down and wavy

Mostly As:

Shawn Johnson

You are most like Olympic gymnast Shawn Johnson. You are petite and have a sparkling personality. Besides being cute as a button, you have determination and drive. You know what you want and you go for it. You love being around your friends and family, and you are a role model in your community. You dress sporty, but with a feminine flare.

Mostly Bs:

Serena Williams

You are most like tennis pro, Serena Williams. You are confident and ambitious, and fight for what's yours. You are strong, dedicated, and passionate. You dress for comfort, and you would play your favorite sport all day every day if it was up to you. You are focused at all times and motivate your friends to do great things. You excel in everything you do.

Mostly Cs:

Jenn Brown

You are most like softball player, Jenn Brown. Not only are you a great athlete, you are beautiful and stylish. You enjoy keeping your body fit because you like to show it off. You are the perfect mix of female and competitive energy, and you make friends easily. You have many admirers and are the focal point of every party. You work hard and play hard.

How sporty are you?

Are sports your life, or an unnecessary annoyance? Whether you are the star of the team or the biggest fan on the sidelines, take this quiz to determine how sporty you really are!

1 How fast can you run 100 yards?
   a. 10 seconds or less
   b. 13-15 seconds
   c. Not sure. A long time?

2 What do you wear for gym class?
   a. Running shoes
   b. Hiking shoes
   c. Flip-flops

3 Your go-to accessory is a:
   a. Basketball
   b. Headband
   c. Bow

4 If you had to choose one sport to play forever it would be:

a. Soccer

b. Swimming

c. Cheerleading

5 Who is your sports idol?

a. Maya Moore

b. Shawn Johnson

c. I don't really have one.

6 Your hair is always:

a. Pulled back

b. In pigtails

c. Curled

7 What do you wish your school would get?

a. New uniforms for the teams.

b. A track

c. New curtains for the stage.

8 How would you describe your body?
a. Muscular
b. Lean
c. Uncoordinated

9 What is your favorite sports movie?
a. *Prefontaine*
b. *For Love of the Game*
c. *Cool Runnings*

10 In gym class you are picked:
a. First!
b. In the top 10.
c. I usually skip gym class.

Mostly As:

Super Sporty: You live, eat, and breathe sports! Always first picked in gym class, you are also the star of the basketball, soccer, and softball teams! Your dream is to play a sport in college, and you are working hard to get a scholarship. You don't care much about trendy clothes or makeup, and you get along much better with guys than girls in your class. You even exercise when you don't have a game or practice. You are super sporty!

Mostly Bs:

Natural Athlete: You have an athletic build and aren't too shabby when it comes to certain sports. You enjoy hiking, jogging, walking, and swimming when you are outside of school. You played sports when you were little, but enjoy solo activities over team sports now. You are one of the first females picked in gym class and you make it a point to watch football with your family every Sunday in the fall. You are a natural athlete.

Mostly Cs:

Not Your Thing: Sports? No way. Whether you find them boring or difficult, these activities have just never appealed to you. That's why you joined the band, art club, and drama club. You couldn't tell the difference between one famous athlete from another, and you only watch a professional sport on TV when forced. Sports just aren't your thing, but you have plenty of other interests and talents to keep you busy anyway.

What kind of boy is right for you?

Boys. We can't live with them, we can't live without them! It's hard to find the right one, but once you do, you'll know it. Take this quiz to help you decide what kind of boy is right for you.

1 **What quality do you admire most in a guy?**
   a. Humor
   b. A "who cares?" attitude
   c. Athleticism

2 **What do you want your future husband to wear to work?**
   a. Anything that makes him comfortable
   b. Jeans
   c. A suit

3 **In school, he is most likely to be voted:**
   a. Class Clown
   b. Most Daring
   c. Prom King

4 He has:

a. Tons of friends

b. Many acquaintances

c. A few close friends, and many admirers.

5 If he were an instrument, he'd be a:

a. Bongo drum

b. Electric guitar

c. Piano

6 On your first date, he:

a. Brings you a flower

b. Picks you up on his motorcycle.

c. Opens the door for you.

7 Your parents:

a. Think he's silly.

b. Worry about him.

c. Love him!

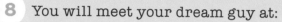

8 You will meet your dream guy at:
   a. A comedy show
   b. Detention
   c. The gym

9 What does he wear to prom?
   a. An orange suit
   b. A leather jacket
   c. A full tux

10 He dances:
   a. By doing the robot.
   b. Only to slow songs.
   c. During group dances.

BOYS
ANSWERS!

Mostly As:

The Class Clown: You love a good laugh so it's important that you find a guy who can tickle your funny bone! You tend to be on the shy side, so you appreciate a guy who can break the ice with a joke. He's smart, quick-witted, and fun, and makes you feel even more special when he chooses to spend time with you over the other girls. Ideal dates for you two would be going to carnivals, going bowling, and, of course, seeing the latest comedy flick.

Mostly Bs:

A Daring Bad Boy: There is nothing more attractive to you than a guy who is not afraid to be himself. You're attracted to daring bad boys because they draw you out of your shell. You get a rush when you're around him and he makes you feel like there is no one else in the world. Just be careful—harmless pranks are fine, but you might get hurt hanging around someone who is dangerous or unpredictable.

Mostly Cs:

The All American Cutie: As cuddly as a teddy bear, the all American cutie is your dream guy. He's polite, a gentleman, athletic, tall, and, of course, handsome. He might be the captain of the football team, the class president, or your lab partner, but he's a born leader. You can bring him home to your parents and rely on him through thick and thin. He considers your feelings and makes you feel special, no matter what. This type of guy is loyal and sweet—definitely a keeper.

Food

- **You would you rather eat:**
  ☐ Leftover pizza ☐ PB&J

- **Tastiest ice cream flavor:**
  ☐ Cookies & cream ☐ Mint & chip ☐ Chocolate

- **Which holiday food do you look forward to?**
  ☐ Mashed potatoes ☐ Turkey ☐ Corn

- **Salad is:**
  ☐ Yummy! ☐ Too healthy

- **What do you snack on more?**
  ☐ Chips ☐ Candy

- **Fast food you crave most:**
  ☐ McDonald's ☐ Taco Bell ☐ Carl's Jr.

- **Your cookie of choice:**
  ☐ Chocolate chip ☐ Macadamia nut ☐ Snickerdoodle

You are:
☐ A picky eater   ☐ Willing to try anything once

How do you feel about sushi?
☐ Yuck!   ☐ Can't wait to try it!   ☐ De-licious!

If you had to choose you'd pick:
☐ Fish   ☐ Chicken   ☐ Tofu

Soda you'd rather drink:
☐ Dr. Pepper   ☐ Coke

Which do you like more?
☐ Hamburger   ☐ Hotdog

Birthday cake:
☐ White   ☐ Chocolate   ☐ Ice Cream

Favorite chocolate?
☐ Dark   ☐ Milk   ☐ White

You would rather eat:
☐ Something sweet   ☐ Something salty

Are you ready to date?

Dating is a big step. You need to make sure that you are ready to handle your emotions and certain social situations. Take this quiz to help you decide if you are ready to date.

1 You go on your first date. You expect him to:

   a. Tell you he had a good time the following day at school.

   b. Call you to set up another date soon.

   c. Do most of the talking.

2 On a date you think he should:

   a. Open the door for you.

   b. Bring you flowers.

   c. Ask you lots of questions.

3 You see his ex while out on a date. You:

   a. Tell him to go say hello.

   b. Shrug it off.

   c. Get very quiet.

4 Who should pay on a date?

    a. You both take turns.

    b. Him most of the time.

    c. Him all of the time.

5 He doesn't call you when he says he will. You:

    a. Think he's just busy.

    b. Think he's tired.

    c. Think he forgot.

6 What is your ideal date?

    a. Dinner

    b. Mini golf

    c. A movie

7 When you are on a date at a restaurant, you:

    a. Eat!

    b. Pick at a salad.

    c. Sip on ice water.

8 He really wants to see a movie but you don't. You:

   a. Go anyway—it's only fair.

   b. Go to the movie and pretend you like it.

   c. Cancel the date.

9 Why do you want to date your crush?

   a. You are crazy about him.

   b. He makes you laugh.

   c. You want to get to know him better.

10 Your after-school activities include:

   a. Shopping with the girls.

   b. Watching his football practice.

   c. Reading and writing poems.

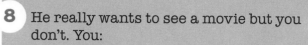

DATING ANSWERS!

Mostly As

100% Ready! You are considered mature for your age and are ready and willing to take on the feelings and responsibilities that come with dating. You are able to open yourself up to someone else, letting them into your life and showing them who you truly are without holding back. You understand that it is important to spend time together but also apart. Most importantly, you know that an ideal couple respects each other's feelings.

75% Ready! You are almost there! While boys love you, you're still trying to find out who you are, and there's nothing wrong with that! In fact, girls that are the most comfortable with themselves tend to have the strongest relationships because they don't get clingy, jealous, or change themselves for a guy. Don't rush things. Stay active with your girls and you will be even more attractive to your crush because you'll show him you have your own life and interests!

Less than 50% Ready! Not yet, but that's okay! You are still trying to decide who you are and what type of guys you like. You get nervous around your crushes and you don't act like yourself, which prohibits them from getting to know the real fabulous you. Instead of worrying about dating, make hanging out with your friends and working on your self-esteem your top priority for a while. Then, you will become happy and confident when it comes to dating your ideal crush!

Which dance style should you learn?

Your dance moves say a lot about you. Make the right statement at your next school dance by taking this quiz – it will help you decide which dance style you should learn!

1 One word that describes you is:
   a. Elegant
   b. Cool
   c. Fun

2 How coordinated are you?
   a. Very coordinated!
   b. Who needs coordination?
   c. You can follow a routine.

3 Your shoe choice is:
   a. Heels
   b. Sneakers
   c. Boots

4 What would you wear to a dance?

a. A long gown

b. A short dress

c. Jeans

5 Your music genre of choice is:

a. Classical

b. R&B

c. Country

6 How do you usually wear your hair?

a. In a tight bun

b. Pulled back

c. In loose waves

7 Will you dance on the floor alone?

a. No, you need a partner.

b. Yes, you love attention.

c. Not without your girls.

8 **Have you ever been in a dance-off?**
  a. No, never!
  b. Yes, I had the freshest moves!
  c. Yes, it was fun!

9 **At a dance you prefer:**
  a. Slow songs
  b. Fast songs
  c. Group line dances

10 **You would like to live in:**
  a. Europe
  b. New York City
  c. Texas

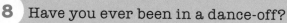

DANCE STYLE ANSWERS!

Mostly As:

Ballroom Dancing: You are chic, elegant, and always sophisticated. Why not learn how to ballroom dance? The Jive, Waltz, and Tango will impress others on the dance floor—especially if you have a handsome willing partner to learn with you! You consider yourself very coordinated and you view dance as a form of art and expression. Ballroom dancing will show off your natural grace and rhythm.

Hip Hop: You are funky, fresh, and cool; your dance should reflect your personality. Moving fluidly and effortlessly will feel like second nature to you on the dance floor. You are determined and athletic enough to even throw in a few break-dance moves into your dance sequence, which will surely wow all of your friends!

Line Dancing: You are a down-home, natural gal who likes to have a good time with your girlfriends on a dance floor. Why not get your cowgirl boots moving by learning and leading a country line dance? The ultimate attention-getter, line dancing shows off your carefree personality and fun-loving, addictive energy. Plus, you'll get the whole crowd moving!

What's your best quality?

We all have something about us that makes us proud. Whether you think you are kind, loyal, funny, or smart; take this quiz to help you define *your* best quality.

1 **What is your favorite type of movie?**
   a. Mystery
   b. Comedy
   c. Action Film
   d. Romantic Comedy

2 **Which school club appeals to you?**
   a. Honor Society
   b. Drama Club
   c. Band
   d. School Spirit Club

3 **You get in an argument with a friend. You:**
   a. Apologize for being right.
   b. Laugh it off.
   c. Send flowers.
   d. Must be dreaming. You never fight with anyone.

4 Who do you sit with at lunch?

  a. Students in your advanced classes.

  b. The jokesters!

  c. Your friends since kindergarten.

  d. Whoever you see sitting alone.

5 You often hear that you are:

  a. Intelligent

  b. Funny

  c. Supportive

  d. Cheerful

6 Which community service project would you take on?

  a. Reading to children.

  b. Putting on a free comedy show.

  c. Assisting the elderly.

  d. A food drive for the homeless.

7 You are stuck in traffic, what do you do?

  a. Calculate a way around it.

  b. Laugh and make the best of it.

  c. Wait it out.

  d. Let others merge in front of you.

8 A fun out-of-school activity is:

  a. Playing cards.

  b. Reading comic books.

  c. Shopping with friends.

  d. Donating things to charity.

9 What do you want to be when you grow up?

  a. A doctor

  b. A movie star

  c. A therapist

  d. A teacher

10 Which candy best describes you?

  a. Smarties

  b. Laffy Taffy

  c. Hershey's Kiss

  d. Skittles

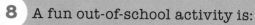

BEST QUALITY ANSWERS!

Mostly As

Smarty Pants! You are intelligent! Your wits are a combination of hard work and a natural gift. You plan to use your knowledge to have an impressive career, perhaps as a doctor or a lawyer. You have a tremendous amount of expertise which makes you interesting, and you frequently impart your vast knowledge with friends. You tutor those who are struggling and take pride in your near perfect test scores and projects in school.

Mostly Bs

Funny Gal! You sure know how to make others laugh. Your best quality is being hilarious. You know how to use just the right amount of wit and sarcasm in a conversation, and others come to you for the latest jokes and comebacks. You lift people's sprits when they are down, and make everyone around you happy. They say laughter is the best medicine, and you are the perfect gal to prescribe it!

Mostly Cs

Loyal Lady! You are incredibly loyal! When you make a friend, it's for life. You always have your loved ones' backs, no matter what. As a result you're well-liked and people trust you. You sometimes put other's needs before your own, and try to avoid confrontation and arguments. You stop any rumors that are spreading, and never hesitate to tell your friends the truth.

Mostly Ds

Kind Soul! Kind is an understatement. You are so good hearted in nature, you don't have any enemies (or even frenemies!). You have nothing but the best intentions in mind for all who come in contact with you, and always have something pleasant and complimentary to say. Your smile is contagious, and you spread cheer to all wherever you go!

Fashion

❋ **When swimming you prefer:**
☐ Bikini ☐ One-piece ☐ Board shorts

❋ **Where would you rather shop?**
☐ Hollister ☐ Justice for Girls

❋ **Your favorite accessory is a:**
☐ Hat ☐ Scarf ☐ Piece of jewelry

❋ Which would you rather wear?
☐ Cowboy hat ☐ Baseball cap ☐ Bandana

❋ **Oversized T-shirts are:**
☐ Great any time of day ☐ Only to sleep in

❋ How would you describe your style?
☐ Sporty ☐ Punk ☐ Chic

❋ **What would you rather wear?**
☐ Tennis shoes ☐ Heels ☐ Flip flops

What do you rock at school?
☐ Skirt ☐ Skinny pants

You would rather wear:
☐ A tutu ☐ A leotard ☐ Flip-flops

When it comes to trends you're:
☐ Creating them ☐ Last to know

Whose style do you like best?
☐ Vanessa Hudgens ☐ Miley Cyrus

Who has better hair?
☐ Justin Bieber ☐ Zac Efron

How often do you change your hairstyle?
☐ All the time ☐ Never

How many times a day do you change your outfit?
☐ 3-4 times at least! ☐ Only when mom makes me

What makes you happier?
☐ New clothes ☐ New accessories

What type of book would your life make?

Books often reflect our lives and the people (or characters!) in them. Take this quiz to determine what kind of book would best sum up your life.

1 What school activity is most appealing to you?
- a. Drama Club
- b. School Spirit Club
- c. Scholastic Scrimmage

2 Your parents are:
- a. Divorced
- b. Happily Married
- c. Famous

3 At a party you are most likely to:
- a. Get into an argument!
- b. Make everyone laugh!
- c. Entertain others with your stories.

4 Where have you traveled?

a. Around town

b. A few places

c. Everywhere

5 What will you end up driving?

a. A used car

b. A VW Bug

c. A BMW

6 You like guys who are:

a. Edgy

b. Funny

c. Well-rounded

7 What is your hobby?

a. Writing in your journal.

b. Practicing magic tricks.

c. Photography

8 Your self-esteem level is:
   a. Low
   b. Moderate
   c. High

9 Do you fight with friends?
   a. Often
   b. Not often
   c. It's a part of life.

10 Your favorite quote is:
   a. "When it rains, it pours."
   b. "Laugh often."
   c. "Work hard, play hard."

BOOK ANSWERS!

Mostly As:

Drama Your life tends to be very dramatic. Things have been up and down, and you are a unique and strong person because of that. You've learned to make the best out of any situation, no matter how frustrating or tragic. While life is full of surprises, with every rainstorm a rainbow is waiting to shine through. So don't worry, be happy now!

Mostly Bs:

Comedy Your life is most like a comedy. All you can do is laugh at what life throws at you. You take everything with a grain of salt and have had dozens of embarrassing moments in your life that are simply hilarious now. You are witty, sarcastic, and surrounded by friends who love to pull pranks and play practical jokes.

Mostly Cs:

Best-seller Your life is most like a best-seller. You have lived through some amazing events that few people get to experience. You are popular, funny, smart, and dramatic, all wrapped into one exciting package. You always have something interesting to discuss and there is something unique about you that others are drawn to.

What's your self confidence level?

Do you feel good about who you are? Are you able to be yourself around your crush and friends? See if you're in need of a confidence boost now with this quick quiz!

1 You know the answer to a question. You:

a. Promptly raise your hand.

b. Answer hesitantly.

c. Do nothing. What if you're wrong?

2 Your prom dress is:

a. The latest trend

b. A neutral tone

c. You don't go to prom.

3 Would you ever wear leopard skin?

a. In a heartbeat!

b. Maybe around friends.

c. Never!

4 A guy compliments you. You:
a. Say thanks!
b. Pretend you don't hear him.
c. Think it's a joke.

5 How do you feel before a class presentation?
a. Calm
b. Nervous
c. Terrified

6 Your go-to sport is:
a. Cheerleading
b. Soccer
c. Chorus

7 You are most likely to be voted:
a. Most Opinionated
b. Best Team Player
c. Quietest Girl

8 **Which color do you prefer?**
a. Yellow
b. Blue
c. Gray

9 **What do you wear at the beach?**
a. A tiny bikini
b. A tankini
c. A tank and shorts

10 **You drop your pencil in class. You:**
a. Get up and get it.
b. Wait until class is over to get it.
c. Pretend it didn't happen.

Mostly As: 10 - Sky High! You are who you are and that's all there is to it. You are not afraid to walk into a party alone, be the first one out on the dance floor, or wear that one-of-a-kind outfit to school. Others look at you as a trendsetter and wish they could be as daring as you. You are not afraid to speak your mind because you feel strong about certain issues, and don't back down when someone challenges you. Your confidence level is sky high!

Mostly Bs: 6 - Mid-Range! You like attention when you get it, but don't go out of your way to attract it. You tend to blend into social situations and are a tad on the quiet side around people you don't know. You'd never dance on a dance floor alone, and you like team sports because you blend in with everyone else! You are confident in certain situations, but could certainly amp it up. Remember—you are an awesome, unique gal!

Mostly Cs: 3 - Too Low! You need a bit of a confidence boost. Others need to see your wonderful, sparkling personality. Let your close friends help you break out of your shell so can show the world just how awesome you are. Try joining a club that caters to your talents and interests so you can shine in the limelight. And if you have something to say, speak up—people will respect you for it.

Which *Hunger Games* character are you?

Even though the *Hunger Games* series is purely fictional, it's filled with characters that you can relate to and connect with. Take this quiz to help you decide which *Hunger Games* character you are most like.

1 If someone picks on your sibling you:
   a. Fight for them!
   b. Embarrass them!
   c. Report it to someone!
   d. Make a plan to get them back!

2 Which word best describes you?
   a. Protective
   b. Creative
   c. Sophisticated
   d. Sly

3 What is your fashion style?
   a. Functional
   b. Stylish
   c. Glamorous
   d. Casual

4 If you were an animal, you'd be a:

   a. Lion

   b. Peacock

   c. Giraffe

   d. Fox

5 How would you describe your family life?

   a. Challenged

   b. Harmonious

   c. Privileged

   d. Dramatic

6 If you could play a sport, you'd choose:

   a. Archery

   b. Ice skating

   c. Cheerleading

   d. Fencing

7 If you were lost in the woods, you'd:

   a. Be able to find a way out.

   b. Be in big trouble.

   c. Be found by a search party.

   d. Be able to survive.

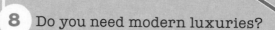

8 Do you need modern luxuries?
   a. No, not at all.
   b. Some, not all.
   c. Yes, of course!
   d. Probably!

9 What is your go-to snack?
   a. Berries
   b. Fish
   c. Steak
   d. Nuts

10 What is your signature accessory?
   a. A hair band
   b. A wig
   c. Feather boa
   d. Sunglasses

HUNGER GAMES ANSWERS!

Mostly As:

Katniss:

Brave, determined, strong, and a survivor; you are the picture of an independent female. You are quick-witted and can keep your cool even in the most intense situations. You tend to protect others and put their needs before your own. You are never afraid to take chances.

Mostly Bs:

Cinna:

You are creative and glamorous—a true fashionista. You have a passion for life and are a carefree, daring soul. You encourage others to relax and be themselves no matter what, because you don't ever pretend to be anyone but yourself.

Mostly Cs:

Effie:

Strong, sophisticated, and powerful, you live a life of privilege. You have the best of the best, but are still able to cut loose and enjoy yourself. You don't take life too seriously and are said to have a comical personality. However, you tend to stress over non-important manners.

Mostly Ds:

Foxface:

You are sly, clever, and smart as a whip like Foxface. You do what you need to do in order to get by, and don't worry about consequences. A rebel to the core, you are edgy, wild, and daring. You don't respect authority, nor do you fear it! Your cleverness will help you out of most difficult situations.

Music

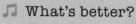

♫ **What's better?**
☐ Country ☐ Rap

♫ **What's more fun to dance to?**
☐ Hip Hop ☐ Pop

♫ **How many songs are on your iTunes?**
☐ Less than 10 ☐ At least 100!

♫ **Who's more fun to sing along to?**
☐ Beyonce ☐ Rihanna

♫ **Classical music or jazz?**
☐ Classical music ☐ Jazz

♫ **Which instrument would you rather play?**
☐ Saxophone ☐ Piano ☐ Guitar

♫ **You would rather:**
☐ Sing in a choir ☐ Play in a band

♫ **Justin Bieber is:**
☐ Super talented (and pretty cute) ☐ OK

♫ **Who would you rather see in concert?**
☐ Zac Efron ☐ Jonas Brothers

♫ **Who has better vocals?**
☐ Miley Cyrus ☐ Ashley Tisdale

♫ **Reality show you'd rather go on:**
☐ *American Idol* ☐ *The Voice*

♫ **Who's a better judge?**
☐ Simon Cowell ☐ Christina Aguilera

♫ **What's more fun to play?**
☐ Flute ☐ Harmonica

♫ **Concerts are:**
☐ A lot of fun! ☐ Never been

♫ **Ever sing in public?**
☐ All the time! ☐ Not in this lifetime

What Greek mythological character are you?

Greek mythological characters are mysterious, interesting, and powerful. They are all very different, so take this quiz to help you decide which Greek character you're most like.

1 You are most likely to be voted:
a. Prom Queen
b. Drama Queen
c. Most Athletic
d. Most Organic

2 How would you describe your style?
a. Feminine
b. Bold
c. Comfortable
d. Natural

3 What is your favorite type of music?
a. Classical
b. Pop
c. Alternative
d. Folk

4 Growing up you played with:

  a. Dolls
  b. Makeup
  c. A basketball
  d. Your garden

5 What do you do with your crush?

  a. Flirt with him.
  b. Ask him out.
  c. Tease him.
  d. Wait for him to make a move.

6 When you grow up, you want to be:

  a. A model
  b. An actor
  c. An athlete
  d. An environmentalist

7 Your go-to hair accessory is a:

  a. Bow
  b. Bold headband
  c. Hair tie
  d. Live flower

8 Which color do you like best?

    a. Pink

    b. Black

    c. Blue

    d. Green

9 Your favorite class in school is:

    a. Art

    b. English

    c. Gym

    d. Horticulture

10 You like guys that are:

    a. Handsome

    b. Funny

    c. Athletic

    d. Smart

Mostly As

Aphrodite: You are beautiful, charming, and captivating. Every guy in your school has had a crush on you at one time or another. You like to be in love and feel most happy when others are in love around you. You're also sly and clever when you need to be, and get your way most of the time.

Mostly Bs

Andromeda: You have a tendency to be dramatic and crave constant attention. After all, you have a very colorful personality that others find captivating. You are passionate, driven, and always speak your mind. And, whenever you put that mind to a task, you can usually accomplish it!

Mostly Cs

Artemis: You are tough, athletic, and very independent. You play every sport well, and are also as smart as a whip. You set goals and accomplish them quickly. People admire your strength and tenacity. You enjoy leading teams to victory and you aren't afraid to get your hands dirty.

Mostly Ds

Gaea: You wear and eat nothing but organic products due to a deep love for the environment. You're a free spirit who believes in making each moment count. However, you like doing things in your own time, so you tend to procrastinate when it comes to studying. That's OK though, things always seem to work out for you.

What meal are you?

You are what you eat. So what meal are you?
Take this quiz and find out!

1 You are mostly likely to be voted:

a. All American Girl

b. Most Likely to Succeed

c. Most Green

d. Most Daring

2 What is your favorite type of food?

a. Italian

b. Seafood

c. Organic

d. Mediterranean

3 Would you ever eat squid?

a. Never, that's gross!

b. Maybe!

c. No, I don't eat meat.

d. Definitely!

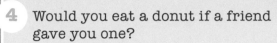

4 Would you eat a donut if a friend gave you one?

   a. Yum, yes please!

   b. If it was a certain brand.

   c. Not a chance.

   d. Yes, if it was unique.

5 Your favorite cereal is:

   a. Captain Crunch

   b. Kashi Go Lean

   c. Granola

   d. Special K Almond and Pecan

6 At lunch you eat:

   a. A sandwich

   b. Salmon

   c. A veggie wrap

   d. Gourmet pizza

7 Your after-school activities include:

   a. Hanging out with friends

   b. Shopping

   c. Rescuing animals

   d. Band practice

8 Your favorite holiday is:
   a. Thanksgiving
   b. Christmas
   c. Arbor Day
   d. Valentine's Day

9 Would you ever eat at a fast food place?
   a. Of course!
   b. Only if you were starving.
   c. Never!
   d. Anything's possible.

10 You can be described as:
   a. Simple
   b. Luxurious
   c. Spiritual
   d. Original

Mostly As:

Spaghetti and Meatballs: You are classic and traditional. You like simplicity and freshness, not things with a lot of bells and frills. You have confidence when it comes to your looks and are proud of who you are. You have many friends, are loud and outgoing, and well-liked by all who meet you!

Mostly Bs:

Surf and Turf: You have a taste for the finer things in life. You are sophisticated and chic. You love to treat yourself to something extravagant every now and then. You work hard and think education is key to a successful future. You always try to look your best wherever you go!

Mostly Cs:

Wedge Salad: You are very spiritual and have a deep a connection with the Earth. You celebrate nature in all its forms. You are all about being organic and conserving resources. You are friendly and honest, and your friends learn a lot from you!

Mostly Ds:

Goat Cheese Pizza: You are a quirky cutie! You aren't afraid to march to the beat of your own drummer, and others admire you for that. You tend to stand out in a crowd (in a good way), and provide new spins on old traditions. You are brave, full of confidence, and aren't afraid to speak your mind!

What will you be when you grow up?

You think about it all the time, but now it's closer than ever before—choosing a career! Take this quiz to help you decide what you should be when you grow up!

1 Who are you most comfortable around?
a. Children
b. Peers
c. Crowds
d. Friends

2 When you walk into a party you:
a. Say hi as you pass others.
b. Talk to one person at a time.
c. Loudly announce your arrival.
d. Stay by your best friend.

3 You have a big presentation. You:
a. Pass out candy before it.
b. Prepare and practice for weeks.
c. Wing it!
d. Get very nervous.

4 Where can you be found hanging out?
- a. The football field
- b. The biology lab
- c. The theater
- d. The library

5 Quality that best describes you:
- a. Patient
- b. Direct
- c. Funny
- d. Quiet

6 What is your least favorite subject in school?
- a. Woodshop
- b. Gym
- c. Math
- d. Reading

7 Do you want children some day?
- a. Yes, lots!
- b. Maybe one!
- c. No, not for me!
- d. Yes, two!

8 How do you work best?
a. With lots of noise
b. In a small setting
c. In a large group
d. On your own

9 You want to be:
a. Happy in life
b. Able to make a difference
c. Rich and famous
d. Peaceful and successful

10 Do you watch the news?
a. Yes, it's important!
b. When you have free time.
c. Nah, boring!
d. Usually!

PROFESSIONS ANSWERS!

Mostly As

Teacher: You love children and you always have. You are able to explain things in a way that everyone can understand. You are compassionate, friendly, caring, and patient. You study and work hard but can also cut back and enjoy yourself. You have a way with people and a positive energy that everyone can't help but notice.

Mostly Bs

Doctor: You are quiet but extremely intelligent. You like to keep to yourself and focus on achieving the many goals you have set for yourself. All you have ever wanted to do was help others, especially those who are sick. You understand theories and complex information. You are great with formulas, symptoms, and enjoy working with your hands.

Mostly Cs

Actress: You are outgoing and you love to stand out in a crowd. Your life can be a little dramatic sometimes, but you wouldn't have it any other way. You have a huge amount of confidence and are multi-talented. In addition to being an amazing singer and dancer, you're also beautiful and glamorous to boot!

Mostly Ds

Accountant: Numbers are your thing. You prefer to work alone, use formulas, and generate lists. You like to complete one task at a time, and you pay attention to the fine details that many people overlook. You are musically inclined because you understand the connection between math and music. Being great at math and science comes naturally to you.

Miscellaneous

Your parents are:
- [ ] So embarrassing
- [ ] So fun!
- [ ] Your heros

Mac or PC?
- [ ] Mac
- [ ] PC

Which is better?
- [ ] Puppies
- [ ] Kittens

Ever been in love?
- [ ] Yes
- [ ] No
- [ ] Maybe

What's scarier?
- [ ] Spiders
- [ ] Snakes

What's worse?
- [ ] Broken arm
- [ ] Broken leg

Which game is better?
- [ ] Monopoly
- [ ] Pictionary

Who do you dread more?
☐ Doctor ☐ Dentist

You'd rather have a:
☐ Yacht ☐ Private jet

Would you rather:
☐ Publish a book ☐ Make a movie

Game system you prefer:
☐ Xbox ☐ Playstation ☐ Wii

What do you play more often?
☐ Board games ☐ Video games

You'd rather get:
☐ Flowers ☐ Love letter

What's cooler?
☐ Piercing ☐ Tattoo

You'd rather live:
☐ On a boat ☐ In a treehouse

Are you a drama mama?

Do you demand attention or just want to blend in? Take this quiz to help you decide if you are a drama mama!

1 You fall in the hallway at school. You:
   a. Cry and scream!
   b. Go straight to the nurse.
   c. Blush but shake it off.

2 What would you do if you got dumped by your boyfriend?
   a. Embarrass him on Facebook.
   b. Start a rumor about him.
   c. Ignore him.

3 You get grounded. You:
   a. Break a picture frame.
   b. Yell at your parents.
   c. Patiently wait it out.

4 Which is your dog of choice?
   a. A Pomeranian
   b. A Pug
   c. A Bulldog

5 If you get a present you hate, you:
   a. Demand it be returned.
   b. Say thanks but sulk.
   c. Pretend you love it.

6 What is your favorite holiday?
   a. Halloween
   b. Thanksgiving
   c. Independence Day

7 If you could be a candy,
   you'd be a:
   a. Hot Tamale
   b. Lemonhead
   c. Hershey's Kiss

8 If you got a flat tire, you would:

a. Make a scene until you get help.

b. Cry and call your parents.

c. Calmly call for a tow truck.

9 You forget your lunch money. You:

a. Beg for a free lunch.

b. Pick at your friends' lunches.

c. Do without it for the day.

10 How would you describe your prom dress?

a. Huge and puffy

b. Short and tight

c. Silky and neutral

DRAMA MAMA ANSWERS!

Mostly As:

Absolutely! Drama is your middle name. You make it a point to stand out and get attention everywhere you go – from school, to home... even the grocery store! While your confidence level is fabulously high, you can sometimes scare people away with all the commotion. Try to relax and keep in mind not *everything* is about you.

Mostly Bs:

From Time to Time! You have your moments, but for the most part you are relatively calm. You enjoy attention when you get it, but don't go out of your way to attract it. You realize when you've gone too far with something, and quickly put the brakes on. Overall, you are very likeable and attract others with your wit and charm.

Mostly Cs:

Never! Drama is something you can do without. In fact, you tend to gravitate toward those who are exactly like you – drama free! You see no need to overreact, and get annoyed when others do. People are attracted to your calm, soothing personality. You are able to control your emotions and are very mature for your age!

What's your hair personality?

What is your hair personality? Does it set itself apart from the rest of the pack? Does it like to play coy and simple, or does it change with your mood? Take this quiz to find out what your hairdo is saying about you.

1 ## What hair color speaks to you?
a. Shocking pink
b. Golden brown
c. Midnight black

2 ## What is your preferred quick hair change technique?
a. Funky hat
b. Messy ponytail
c. Bun

3 ## What is your favorite hair length?
a. Wispy and pixie
b. Long and straight with neat bangs
c. Molded and sculpted

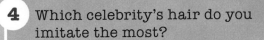

4 Which celebrity's hair do you imitate the most?
   a. Rihanna
   b. Kristen Stewart
   c. Jennifer Aniston

5 What kind of hair accessory would you wear?
   a. Big feather barrette
   b. Fresh flower behind your ear
   c. Bobby pins for a big updo

6 What do you do when you have a bad hair day?
   a. Decide you need a new haircut
   b. Braid it
   c. Go with it

7 Where do you regularly get your hair done?
   a. Beauty college
   b. A trusted hairstylist
   c. Trendy salon

8 What's more important?

a. Rocking a standout hairstyle

b. Getting a look your friends will imitate

c. Keeping a healthy, simple mane

9 What one thing would you change about your hair?

a. The color

b. Make it longer

c. Not much, maybe a light trim

10 What would your friends say about your hair?

a. "Wow, I can't keep up with your looks!"

b. "Have you ever considered going blonde?"

c. "Your look is so classic!"

Mostly As:
Risk-taking Tresses

Your hair personality changes constantly, wherever the wind takes it, so to speak. You could never be satisfied with just ONE look—you crave excitement and variety. Look to celebs like Rihanna and Lady Gaga for some ambitious 'do ideas.

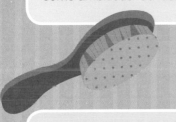

Mostly Bs:
Dramatic Tendrils

You don't go for trends but rather dive right into your inner diva when it comes to your 'do. Dark, long and often in a feature-worthy upsweep, your hairstyle personality demands to be looked at. Try one of Kristen Stewart's famous red carpet looks as your next show-stopping hairdo.

Mostly Cs:
Classic Coif

You rarely have a hair out of place, and it always looks healthy and beautiful. You prefer simplicity over complicated hairstyles. Minimal products are key, the more natural-looking the better. Check out classic beauty Gwyneth Paltrow for soft-style inspiration.

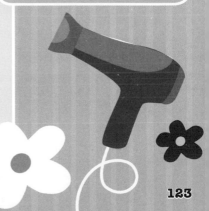